WESTMINSTER SCHOOLS

SMYTHE GAMBRELL
LIBRARY

B.H.

PRESENTED BY

Michael and Mimi Ann Scaljon
1988

SOME MAJOR EVENTS IN WORLD WAR II

THE EUROPEAN THEATER

1939 SEPTEMBER—Germany invades Poland; Great Britain, France, Australia, & New Zealand declare war on Germany; Battle of the Atlantic begins. NOVEMBER—Russia invades Finland.

1940 APRIL—Germany invades Denmark & Norway. MAY—Germany invades Belgium, Luxembourg, & The Netherlands; British forces retreat to Dunkirk and escape to England. JUNE—Italy declares war on Britain & France; France surrenders to Germany. JULY—Battle of Britain begins. SEPTEMBER—Italy invades Egypt; Germany, Italy, & Japan form the Axis countries. OCTOBER—Italy invades Greece. NOVEMBER—Battle of Britain over. DECEMBER—Britain attacks Italy in North Africa.

1941 JANUARY—Allies take Tobruk. FEBRUARY—Rommel arrives at Tripoli. APRIL—Germany invades Greece & Yugoslavia. JUNE—Allies are in Syria; Germany invades Russia. JULY—Russia joins Allies. AUGUST—Germans capture Kiev. OCTOBER—Germany reaches Moscow. DECEMBER—Germans retreat from Moscow; Japan attacks Pearl Harbor; United States enters war against Axis nations.

1942 MAY—first British bomber attack on Cologne. JUNE—Germans take Tobruk. SEPTEMBER—Battle of Stalingrad begins. OCTOBER—Battle of El Alamein begins. NOVEMBER—Allies recapture Tobruk; Russians counterattack at Stalingrad.

1943 JANUARY—Allies take Tripoli. FEBRUARY—German troops at Stalingrad surrender. APRIL—revolt of Warsaw Ghetto Jews begins. MAY—German and Italian resistance in North Africa is over; their troops surrender in Tunisia; Warsaw Ghetto revolt is put down by Germany. JULY—Allies invade Sicily; Mussolini put in prison. SEPTEMBER—Allies land in Italy; Italians surrender; Germans occupy Rome; Mussolini rescued by Germany. OCTOBER—Allies capture Naples; Italy declares war on Germany. NOVEMBER—Russians recapture Kiev.

1944 JANUARY—Allies land at Anzio. JUNE—Rome falls to Allies; Allies land in Normandy (D-Day). JULY—assassination attempt on Hitler fails. AUGUST—Allies land in southern France. SEPTEMBER—Brussels freed. OCTOBER—Athens liberated. DECEMBER—Battle of the Bulge.

1945 JANUARY—Russians free Warsaw. FEBRUARY—Dresden bombed. APRIL—Americans take Belsen and Buchenwald concentration camps; Russians free Vienna; Russians take over Berlin; Mussolini killed; Hitler commits suicide. MAY—Germany surrenders; Goering captured.

THE PACIFIC THEATER

1940 SEPTEMBER—Japan joins Axis nations Germany & Italy.

1941 APRIL—Russia & Japan sign neutrality pact. DECEMBER—Japanese launch attacks against Pearl Harbor, Hong Kong, the Philippines, & Malaya; United States and Allied nations declare war on Japan; China declares war on Japan, Germany, & Italy; Japan takes over Guam, Wake Island, & Hong Kong; Japan attacks Burma.

1942 JANUARY—Japan takes over Manila; Japan invades Dutch East Indies. FEBRUARY—Japan takes over Singapore; Battle of the Java Sea. APRIL—Japanese overrun Bataan. MAY—Japan takes Mandalay; Allied forces in Philippines surrender to Japan; Japan takes Corregidor; Battle of the Coral Sea. JUNE—Battle of Midway; Japan occupies Aleutian Islands. AUGUST—United States invades Guadalcanal in the Solomon Islands.

1943 FEBRUARY—Guadalcanal taken by U.S. Marines. MARCH—Japanese begin to retreat in China. APRIL—Yamamoto shot down by U.S. Air Force. MAY—U.S. troops take Aleutian Islands back from Japan. JUNE—Allied troops land in New Guinea. NOVEMBER—U.S. Marines invade Bougainville & Tarawa.

1944 FEBRUARY—Truk liberated. JUNE—Saipan attacked by United States. JULY—battle for Guam begins. OCTOBER—U.S. troops invade Philippines; Battle of Leyte Gulf won by Allies.

1945 JANUARY—Luzon taken; Burma Road won back. MARCH—Iwo Jima freed. APRIL—Okinawa attacked by U.S. troops; President Franklin Roosevelt dies; Harry S. Truman becomes president. JUNE—United States takes Okinawa. AUGUST—atomic bomb dropped on Hiroshima; Russia declares war on Japan; atomic bomb dropped on Nagasaki. SEPTEMBER—Japan surrenders.

WORLD AT WAR

Nisei Regiment

WORLD AT WAR

Nisei Regiment

By R. Conrad Stein

Consultant:
   Professor Robert L. Messer, Ph.D.
   Department of History
   University of Illinois, Chicago

 CHILDRENS PRESS ™

CHICAGO

These German storm troopers surrendered to members of the 100/442
Regimental Combat Team during a battle in Italy in 1944.

FRONTISPIECE:
A member of the illustrious 100/442 Regimental
Combat Team

PICTURE CREDITS:
NATIONAL ARCHIVES: Cover, pages 10, 20, 21,
25, 27, 39 (bottom right), 46
UPI: Pages 4, 12, 13, 15, 16, 17, 24, (top), 39 (top)
GO FOR BROKE INC./NATIONAL JAPANESE AMERI-
CAN HISTORICAL SOCIETY: Pages 6, 9, 18, 19, 23,
28, 30, 31, 32, 35, 36, 39 (bottom left), 40, 41, 42,
45
WIDE WORLD PHOTOS: Pages 24 (bottom), 34

COVER PHOTO:
Twenty-six hundred Japanese American volunteers from Hawaii attended the ceremony in Hon-
olulu that preceded their departure to the United
States mainland for training at Camp Shelby.

PROJECT EDITOR:
Joan Downing

CREATIVE DIRECTOR:
Margrit Fiddle

**Library of Congress Cataloging in
Publication Data**

Stein, R. Conrad.
  Nisei Regiment.

  (World at war)
  Includes index.
  Summary: A history of the 442nd "Nisei" Regiment which was almost entirely made up of Japanese American men and received more medals for
bravery than any other American unit its size during World War II.
  1. World War, 1939–1945—Regimental histo-
ries—United States—Juvenile literature.
2. United States. Army. Regimental Combat
Team, 442nd—Juvenile literature. 3. World
War, 1939–1945—Campaigns—Europe—Juvenile literature. 4. World War, 1939–1945—Par-
ticipation, Japanese Americans—Juvenile
literature. 5. Japanese Americans—History—
20th century—Juvenile literature.
[1. World War, 1939–1945—Regimental histo-
ries—United States. 2. United States. Army.
Regimental Combat Team, 442nd. 3. World
War, 1939–1945—Campaigns—Europe.
4. Japanese Americans]
I. Title. II. Series.
D769.31. 442nd.S73 1985
940.54'12'73   82-17855
ISBN 0-516-04770-1

Late in World War II, a story circulated among the men of a very special American regiment. The story told of a German rifleman who was under attack. The German saw dim figures coming at him. The figures darted forward, took cover, darted forward, and took cover again. Steadily they advanced, getting closer, closer, closer. The German fired his rifle. Other members of his platoon also opened fire. But the enemy kept pressing the attack. Finally the platoon was surrounded, and the Germans were forced to surrender.

With his hands high in the air, the German rifleman crawled out of his foxhole. Though he was terrified, he still longed for a look at the brave men who had overwhelmed his platoon. The German was astonished to discover that his enemies were Asian.

"You—you Chinese?" the German rifleman asked one of his captors.

"No," said the man, smiling. "We're Japanese. Didn't Hitler tell ya? We switched sides."

The men who told that story were members of the 100/442 Regimental Combat Team. They were a very special unit for two reasons. First, the regiment was made up almost entirely of Japanese American men. Second, the 100/442 received more medals for bravery than any other American unit its size during all of World War II.

The men of the 100/442 won more than 18,000 individual decorations. These included a Congressional Medal of Honor, 560 Silver Stars, 4,000 Bronze Stars, and almost 10,000 Purple Hearts. The regiment suffered the highest casualty rate of any unit in the history of the United States Army. The soldiers endured almost two years of constant combat, but not one of them was ever tried for desertion. In fact, at different times, six wounded members of the regiment sneaked out of their hospital beds to rejoin their buddies at the front.

The 100/442 was the most decorated American unit of World War II.
Above: Colonel Ernst Barco awards the Purple Heart to Private Harry Koka.

Why did these Japanese Americans fight so heroically for their country? That question is hard to answer, for their country certainly did them few favors.

Early in this century, the American people, especially those living on the West Coast, developed a bitter anti-Asian attitude. This feeling about Asians eventually was reflected in laws. In 1922, the United States Supreme Court declared that Japanese were "aliens ineligible to citizenship." In 1924, Congress passed a law virtually prohibiting the further immigration of Japanese people.

After Pearl Harbor, prejudice against Japanese Americans was often openly expressed, as in this sign on the door of a barbershop in Parker, Arizona.

Because of these laws, the word *Nisei* became important to the Japanese living in America. Nisei combines the Japanese words for "two" and "generation." A Nisei is a second-generation Japanese person born in the United States. All Nisei automatically became citizens. But whether they were citizens or not, the Japanese still were regarded with fear and superstition by white Americans. When the United States was plunged into World War II by a Japanese surprise attack on Pearl Harbor, the whites' fear and superstition exploded.

War breeds hatred and hatred breeds injustice. This is an ancient vicious truism. After Pearl Harbor, the day-to-day injustices suffered by Japanese Americans became a nightmare. Signs such as these suddenly appeared on store windows in California, Oregon, and Washington: DIRTY JAP KEEP OUT OF HERE. GO HOME JAP RAT.

Anti-Japanese statements were made in newspapers and in speeches. Writing for a West Coast paper, a reporter named McLemore said: "Why treat Japs well here? I am for the immediate removal of every Japanese. . . . Let them be pinched, hurt, hungry, and dead up against it. . . . Personally, I hate the Japanese." Even high government officials joined the hate crusade. The governor of Idaho said in a speech: "Japs live like rats, breed like rats, and act like rats. We don't want them buying or leasing land and becoming permanently located in our state."

On the day Pearl Harbor was attacked, these Japanese Americans were detained and questioned by the FBI because they lived near the site of a naval base in Los Angeles.

The hatred that West Coast Americans felt toward the Japanese Americans quickly turned into blind, often senseless, fear. Stories spread that people had seen Nisei who lived along the coast signaling Japanese submarines at night. During and after the war, no one could find a scrap of evidence that any Japanese American had aided the Tokyo government. But rumors persisted that all Nisei were spies. Many white Americans suggested that the government round up the Japanese Americans and move them away from the coast.

Despite a complete lack of evidence, Japanese Americans, especially those on the Pacific Coast, were treated as possible spies. Police confiscated shortwave radios and government agents searched homes for signaling devices that might be used to transmit messages to Japanese submarines offshore.

One of those who advocated forcibly removing the Japanese Americans was an army general named John DeWitt. In a letter to the secretary of war that reached heights of illogic, DeWitt wrote: "The Japanese race is an enemy race and while many second and third generation Japanese born on United States soil, possessed of United States citizenship, have become 'Americanized,' the racial strains are undiluted. . . . It therefore follows that along the vital Pacific Coast over 112,000 potential enemies, of Japanese extraction, are at large today. . . . The very fact that no sabotage has taken place to date is a disturbing and confirming indication that such action will be taken."

Four months after Pearl Harbor, President Franklin D. Roosevelt issued an order that all West Coast Japanese Americans must be removed to what were called "relocation camps." General DeWitt was one of the men in charge of the removal. All Japanese had to

The Japanese Americans who were moved to relocation centers had to abandon
their homes, stores (above), and most of their possessions.

go—men and women, babies and old people,
citizens and noncitizens. General DeWitt once
told a congressional committee, "A Jap's a
Jap. It makes no difference whether he is an
American citizen or not."

The relocation centers were barbed-wire
enclaves located in remote areas. In all, some
112,000 people were confined in ten different
camps. The Japanese Americans and their
parents had no trials, no hearings, no due
process of law. They were instantly

Under army escort, the first group of Japanese American technicians—doctors, nurses, and clerks—prepares to leave Los Angeles for a relocation center in Manzanar, California.

dispossessed of their belongings, homes, and other possessions that they could not carry in "their two hands" or within a time period of one day to two weeks. They were taken under guard, as if they were criminals. Locking up American citizens simply because they had Japanese ancestors was one of the most outrageous injustices in the history of the United States. Clearly, racism contributed to the order. In 1942, the United States was also at war with Germany and Italy. Yet no one suggested that Italian Americans and German Americans living on the East Coast be locked up.

At the relocation centers, Japanese Americans were guarded like prisoners.

With many of their relatives imprisoned in barbed-wire camps, the men of the Nisei regiment still became the most decorated United States troops of World War II. Why?

The men of the 100/442 believed they had to fight with extra courage in order to prove that they were just as loyal as any other citizens. "We were fighting for the rights of all Japanese Americans," said 100/442 infantryman Harry Takagi. "We set out to break every record in the army. If we failed, it would reflect discredit on all Japanese Americans. We could not let that happen."

The army requested fifteen hundred Japanese American volunteers from Hawaii; more than ten thousand responded.

The 100/442 grew out of a unit called the 100th Infantry Battalion. The 100th was formed as an experimental outfit just six months after Pearl Harbor. It was made up of Nisei men and white officers. The experiment worked so successfully that on February 1, 1943, the army established a regiment composed solely of Nisei, to be called the 442nd Regimental Combat Team. All the members of the regiment were volunteers. Many were recruited directly from the relocation centers.

The men of the 442nd trained at Camp Shelby, Mississippi. Sometime during their training they adopted the words "Go For Broke" as both their battle cry and their motto.

Lieutenant Masoa Yamada, the first Japanese American to be commissioned a chaplain in the United States Army, reports for duty at Camp Shelby.

Many of the Nisei were from Hawaii, and "going for broke" was an expression used by Hawaiian dice-shooters when they wanted to gamble all of their money on one roll of the dice. The most famous veteran of the 442nd was a young volunteer named Daniel K. Inouye. He later explained what the motto "Go For Broke" meant to the men: "It meant giving everything we had; jabbing every bayonet dummy as though it were the enemy himself, scrambling over an obstacle course as though our lives depended on it; marching quick time until we were ready to drop—and then breaking into a trot."

Determined to prove that they were just as loyal as other Americans, the men of the 442nd trained tirelessly while at Camp Shelby. Right: A private is shown the proper stance for throwing a hand grenade. Below: Recruits are taught self-defense techniques.

Above: Camp Shelby recruits learn how to construct a pontoon (floating) bridge. Below: After a long period of rigorous training, a jeep crew learns that before long they will be needed overseas.

In Mississippi, the Nisei men ran into another problem—segregation in the deep South. At the time, black people were not allowed in most restaurants or movie theaters. Rest rooms and drinking fountains in public places were labeled "white only" or "colored only." How would the southerners treat the thousands of nonwhite Nisei now pouring into Camp Shelby? After much debate, the people of the towns surrounding the camp decided to let the Japanese Americans into their restaurants and stores. For southern white people before the days of civil rights laws, this was an enormous concession.

The United States government, however, never conceded a thing when it concerned the Japanese Americans. Agents of the FBI lurked about the 442nd barracks. When the troops went on leave, they were sometimes followed by FBI men. The agents, looking for spies and saboteurs among the Nisei, found none.

Company E of the 442nd stands at attention during training at Camp Shelby.

Training for the 442nd lasted more than a year. Other army regiments trained for only four to six months before being sent overseas. The 442nd was not shipped overseas sooner because most army commanders still mistrusted large numbers of Nisei troops. This mistrust is difficult to understand, given the record of the first small unit of Nisei to see combat.

General Mark Clark (right), commanding general of the Fifth Army in Italy, was so impressed by the performance of the 100th Battalion (below) that he used it as a spearhead unit on the road to Rome.

In Italy, a private of the 100th Battalion fires a machine gun from tree cover.

The Nisei 100th Infantry Battalion landed at Salerno, Italy, on September 22, 1943, just thirteen days after the Allies had stormed ashore at the beachhead. The battalion remained in the thick of the fight during the long and bloody road to Rome. The 100th fought so bravely that American General Mark Clark used it as a spearhead unit. A spearhead unit always attacks first and is usually thrown at the enemy's toughest troops. The 100th led the way during the arduous crossing of the Rapido River. It was one of the lead units to assault the mountain fortress of Cassino. During every attack, the men of the 100th battled with unbelievable bravery. When General Clark was asked about the loyalty of the Japanese American soldiers under his command, he said only, "Send me more of those men."

Because of the 100th Battalion's bravery, the 442nd finally got its chance to fight.

The "Go For Broke" regiment arrived in Italy in May, 1944. What was left of the 100th Battalion joined them. The 100th had suffered so many casualties that other GIs called it the "Purple Heart Battalion." It had fought so gallantly that the War Department allowed the unit to retain its name. When the 100th joined the 442nd, the unit became known as the 100/442 Regimental Combat Team.

Soldiers of the 100/442 fire a mortar into the hills on the Italian front.

In Italy, the 100/442 became locked in some of the most furious fighting of the war. The Nisei men pushed across the Arno River and captured fifty miles of territory held by units considered to be the best troops in the German army. The Japanese Americans stormed up Hill 140, where the Germans were dug in with such great strength the hill was called "Little Cassino." Averaging two hours of sleep a night, the Nisei men liberated eleven towns and villages in northern Italy. Once on the attack, the men of the regiment never took a backward step or lost a foot of the ground they had won.

In August, 1944, General Clark (left) reviewed the soldiers of the 100/442 Regimental Combat Team, who had just contributed to the successful assault on Leghorn, Italy.

Although the men fought with reckless courage, they knew that war still means killing and is therefore a very dirty business. "I never got used to it," wrote Daniel Inouye. "Deep down I think no one did. We pretended to be calloused and insensitive because we understood the fatal consequence of caring too much."

Mr. Inouye tells this tragic story about finding a wounded German soldier in a bombed-out house: "He reached into his tunic, and I thought he was going for a gun. It was war; you had only one chance to make the right decision. I pumped the last three shots in my rifle clip into his chest. As he toppled over, his hand sprang spasmodically from the tunic, and he held up a snapshot, clutching it in death. It was a picture of a pretty woman and two little children, and there was a handwritten inscription: *'Deine Dichliebende Frau, Hedi.'* So I had made a widow and two orphans."

In October, 1944, the men of the 100/442 had to fight their way through a dense forest in the Vosges Mountains of France to rescue an American battalion surrounded by Germans.

From northern Italy, the 100/442 was transferred to northeastern France. There they fought what was perhaps their most famous battle. In the Vosges Mountains, near the town of Bruyeres, a battalion of infantrymen had been surrounded by the Germans. Most of the men of the battalion were from Texas. For almost a week, the Texans had been cut off and had been supplied by air drops. Their situation was desperate, and the battalion was on the verge of being overrun. The 100/442 was ordered to break the German ring surrounding the Texan troops.

To reach the surrounded battalion, the men of the 100/442 had to fight their way through

As they inched along on their rescue mission, the Japanese Americans were in constant danger of being hit by machine-gun fire or shrapnel from German mortar shells.

a thick forest. It was a brutal tree-by-tree battle. Hidden German machine-gun nests seemed to be everywhere. German artillery and mortar shells exploded when they hit the top branches of trees. The tree bursts were deadly because they sent showers of shrapnel raining down on the Americans. After four days of constant combat, the 100/442 counted two hundred men dead and more than six hundred wounded. But they battered through the German ring and saved the surrounded battalion. The Texans, many of whom disliked or mistrusted Asians, nevertheless hugged the men of the 100/442 as if they were brothers.

During the battle in the Vosges Mountains, medics of the 100/442 carry away a wounded comrade. When the four-day battle to save the surrounded Texan unit was over, two hundred Nisei had been killed and six hundred had been wounded.

After the battle, the general who commanded the Texans wanted to thank the men of the 100/442. He asked the 100/442 commander, Colonel Virgil Miller, to assemble his troops. But at the assembly, the general was shocked to see only a few hundred men. A regiment normally numbers forty-five hundred soldiers. "Where are the rest of the men?" the general asked. With tears in his eyes, Colonel Miller replied, "You're looking at the entire regiment, sir. . . . That's all that's left."

Replacements were brought from the United States to fill the ranks of the battered 100/442. One of them was a young man named George Sawada. In a letter, Sawada described his feelings toward his country after he and his family were imprisoned in a relocation camp: "It was a bitter blow to me. I, a citizen, with a brother already serving in the United States Army, must evacuate, and I could not understand why the German and Italian aliens were not included. I had an unbounding faith in the justice of this nation, but she in return had placed me behind barbed wire like an enemy alien. . . . But when the time came for enlistment I was ready, my faith and loyalty restored, stronger, firmer, unwavering." George Sawada was killed by a sniper's bullet during his first week in combat.

Taking a break from the fighting on the Fifth Army front in Italy, soldiers of the 100/442 stand in line for a well-deserved meal.

From France, the 100/442 was shipped back to Italy in 1945. In Italy, the German forces were commanded by a crafty field marshal named Albert Kesselring. His strategy was to defend Italy by conducting planned retreats into previously prepared defensive lines. So when the Allies pushed the Germans off one mountain range, the enemy simply melted into defensive positions on the next. The Italian campaign lasted twenty grueling months. The Allies had to scratch, crawl, and bleed for every foot of land they gained.

Nisei soldiers approached a German-occupied farmhouse (above) and began cleaning it out (below) during the last campaign of the 100/442 in the Po Valley of Italy in April, 1945.

Medics (background) made their way over a trail to rescue surviving members of the 100/442 after two mortar shells exploded at this spot.

Late in the war, a battle raged at the tiny village of Aulla. Near that village, Daniel K. Inouye led a platoon of 100/442 men. Inouye had enlisted as a private, and worked his way through the ranks to earn a battlefield commission as a second lieutenant.

Inouye's platoon was pinned down by German machine-gun fire. He was wounded, but with a grenade in his hand he crawled up to one of the enemy machine-gun positions.

"And as I drew my arm back, all in a flash of light and dark I saw him, that faceless German, like a strip of motion-picture film running through a projector that's gone berserk. One instant he was standing waist-high in the bunker, and the next he was aiming a rifle grenade at my face from a range of ten yards. And even as I cocked my arm to throw, he fired and his rifle grenade smashed into my right elbow and exploded and all but tore my arm off. I looked at it, stunned and unbelieving. It dangled there by a few bloody shreds of tissue, my grenade still clenched in a fist that suddenly didn't belong to me any more."

That battle was the last for Daniel K. Inouye. He killed the German soldier, but what was left of Inouye's arm had to be amputated in a field hospital. Inouye was out of the war for good.

After the battle, the 100/442 was given a well-earned rest. The unit also began to receive recognition for its courage. Some commanders were calling the Nisei troops "America's secret weapon." General Mark Clark said of the "Go For Broke" Regiment, "I am convinced that no wartime commander ever had at his disposal a finer body of fighting men than the 100/442. . . . Their sacrifice in terms of loss of lives, wounds, and general privation cannot be repaid by mere words, but their deeds have won the sincere admiration of Americans." And in 1945, Secretary of War Robert Patterson wrote: "Through the bitter fighting. . . the battle skill, cool bravery, and individual fortitude of these men became legendary to their comrades and the enemy alike."

At home, the American people read about the heroics of the Nisei. Many Americans were overcome by guilt because their country had doubted the loyalty of Japanese Americans.

Above: Decorated Nisei soldiers, looking forward to going home to Hawaii after being wounded in battle, gather around a piano in San Francisco.

Left: At an army hospital, General Clark commends wounded Japanese American soldiers for their bravery in battle.

Below: Private Tsukio Yamagato receives one of the eighteen thousand decorations that were awarded to soldiers of the 100/442.

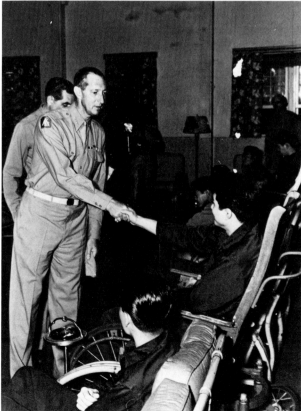

Hawaiian members of the 100/442 received a hero's welcome when they returned home.

Still, the Japanese Americans on the West Coast had remained locked up for almost the entire length of the war. When they were finally released, many found that their homes had been vandalized or sold as abandoned property. For them, the results of a lifetime of work and savings had been wiped out. After the war, thousands of Japanese Americans left the West Coast never to return. They moved to other parts of the country and started new lives.

In Hawaii, still a possession and not yet a state, the circumstances were very different. The Japanese Americans there had never been locked up. They numbered a third of the population of Hawaii—too large a group to imprison. When Hawaiian members of the

The 100/442 produced two United States senators—Daniel K. Inouye (left), and Spark M. Matsunaga (right).

100/442 returned, they received a hero's welcome. About his return to Hawaii, Daniel Inouye wrote: "For a while there was a great, wild spree of homecoming celebrations. Two 100/442 vets meeting on the street was reason enough for a party."

The book Daniel K. Inouye later wrote, which included his experiences in the 100/442, was called *Journey to Washington*. In 1959, Mr. Inouye became Hawaii's first United States representative, and in 1962 he entered the Senate. Serving as Hawaii's other senator was Spark M. Matsunaga, also a veteran of the 100/442. The regiment is the only outfit in the armed forces that ever produced two United States senators.

Although the men of the 100/442 fought only in Europe, about six thousand other Japanese Americans contributed greatly to the war effort in the Pacific, where they were used in secret operations. This Nisei interpreter (center) helped gather information about the enemy by interrogating a captured Japanese officer (right).

The "Go For Broke" Regimental Combat Team fought exclusively in Europe. Would Japanese Americans have fought as fiercely and as loyally against Japan? The answer to that question is an unqualified yes.

Although the 100/442 saw no action in the Pacific, some six thousand Japanese Americans did serve in that theater. During the war, the actions of the Nisei in the Pacific were kept secret. Many of them were involved in spying operations. The United States, of course, did not want the Japanese to know of their existence. But it was Japanese Americans who translated intercepted radio messages and revealed to General Douglas MacArthur the Japanese plan to defend the Philippines. Nisei translators gave the defense plans of Okinawa to the American marine commander. After the war, General Charles Willoughby, who served as MacArthur's chief intelligence officer, stated, "The Nisei saved countless Allied lives and shortened the war by two years."

The contributions of Japanese Americans to the Allied victory in World War II were enormous. Today it is staggering to think that those same Japanese Americans were thought to be spies and were imprisoned in barbed-wire camps.

When the crack troops of the 100/442 returned to the United States from overseas, they went first to Washington, D.C. There President Harry Truman presented to them a special Presidential Unit Citation. Upon giving the award to the "Go For Broke" men, the president said: "I can't tell you how much I appreciate the privilege of being able to show you how much the United States thinks of what you have done. . . . You fought not only the enemy, but you fought prejudice. . . and you won."

To show America's appreciation of the 100/442's accomplishments, President Harry Truman presented the regiment with a special Presidential Unit Citation.

At a memorial service in France in 1944, Chaplain Hgro Higuchi
eulogized Nisei soldiers who had been killed in action.

Index

Page numbers in boldface type indicate illustrations

About the Author

Mr. Stein was born and grew up in Chicago. At eighteen he enlisted in the Marine Corps where he served three years. He was a sergeant at discharge. He later received a B.A. in history from the University of Illinois and an M.F.A. from the University of Guanajuato in Mexico.

Although he served in the Marines, Mr. Stein believes that wars are a dreadful waste of human life. He agrees with a statement once uttered by Benjamin Franklin: "There never was a good war or a bad peace." But wars are all too much a part of human history. Mr. Stein hopes that some day there will be no more wars to write about.

The author wishes to thank the office and staff of Senator Daniel K. Inouye for their cooperation in helping him prepare this book.

834